Tam is in bed. He is napping.

Min is not in bed. She is singing a song.
It is a long song and Tam cannot nap.

Tam gets up and rings Min.
"Stop singing, Min! I am in bed."
Min stops singing. Tam gets back into bed.

Min plucks the strings. Pling! Pling! Pling!
Tam cannot nap.
Tam gets up and rings Min.

"Hush, Min! I am napping."
Min stops plucking the strings.
Tam gets back into bed.

Min rings a bell. Ding! Dong! Ding!
Tam cannot nap.

Tam is cross. He rings Min.
"Stop ringing the bell, Min! Get into bed!"
Min stops ringing the bell. Tam gets back into bed.

Tam is in bed. Min is in bed.
No songs... no strings... no bells.

Tam cannot nap. He rings Min.
"Sing me a song to help me drop off."
"No!" Min tells Tam. "Stop ringing...

...I am in bed!"

Speaking and listening

Who are these characters?

Tam　　Min

Can you read these words?

chips　　froth　　strings　　bench

Spelling and writing

Ask your child to blend and read the words below. Ask them to say each word and to tap out the phonemes (sounds) of the word with their fingers. Then ask your child to try writing each word.

song

them

fish

Understanding the story These questions will help you to check that your child understands the story.

1 Where is Tam? (page 1)

2 What is Min doing? (page 2)

3 What does Tam do next? (page 3)